WITHDRAWN FROM STOCK

D0588311

The Little
Book of
Intentional
Living

The Little
Book of
Intentional
Living

Create the life you want
through the power of intention

Carolyn Boyes

An Hachette UK Company
www.hachette.co.uk

First published in Great Britain in 2019 by Gaia,
an imprint of Octopus Publishing Group Ltd
Carmelite House
50 Victoria Embankment
London EC4Y 0DZ
www.octopusbooks.co.uk

Design and Layout Copyright © Octopus Publishing Group Ltd 2019
Text Copyright © Carolyn Boyes 2019

Distributed in the US by
Hachette Book Group
1290 Avenue of the Americas
4th and 5th Floors
New York, NY 10104

Distributed in Canada by
Canadian Manda Group
664 Annette St., Toronto,
Ontario, Canada M6S 2C8

All rights reserved. No part of this work may be reproduced or utilized in any
form or by any means, electronic or mechanical, including photocopying, recording
or by any information storage and retrieval system, without the prior written
permission of the publisher.

Carolyn Boyes asserts her moral right to be identified as the author of this work.

ISBN 978-1-85675-402-6

A CIP catalogue record for this book is available from the British Library.

Printed and bound in China.

10 9 8 7 6 5 4 3 2 1

Commissioning Editor: Leanne Bryan
Art Director: Juliette Norsworthy
Senior Editor: Pollyanna Poulter
Designer and Illustrator: Abi Read
Copy Editor: Mandy Greenfield
Production Controller: Emily Noto

Contents

Introduction

What is "intentional living"? Intentional living is a simple idea. It is about deciding to live a life that has purpose and is in harmony and alignment with your values. When you live intentionally, you decide what matters to *you*, and you set the direction of your life.

Have you ever noticed how quickly time flies by? Before you know it, a lifetime has passed without you doing or being what you intended. Intentional living is about taking the time to connect with your dreams and desires, determining what you do and don't want in life and then living this way on a daily basis. This idea comes from spiritual traditions, but you don't need to be spiritual to live a life that matters.

When we are born, we have the ability, as human beings, to make conscious choices. A life that looks good to other people is not necessarily a life that *feels* good. A life full of material success is not the measure of happiness. Nor is a busy life a fulfilling one. So many of us live in stress or boredom, not fully present or committed to the life path we are taking. But it doesn't have to be like this.

Intuition: life's instruction manual

Wouldn't it be wonderful if life came with an instruction manual? It does. It's called your intuition.

We are busier than we've ever been before. Emails, social media and other distractions mean that we have busy lives, but not necessarily fulfilling ones. As a result, we have become disconnected from what really matters. It is easy to forget to stop and ask yourself the really important questions. But powerful questions empower you. They open you up to self-knowledge and ensure that you use your own instruction manual to make the right choices for you. Through living intentionally you will become better at listening to your intuition, by asking yourself the right questions and taking the time to hear the answers about what it is that you wish to create in this life.

"There is only one time when it is essential to awaken. That time is now."

BUDDHA

What are intentions?

Intentions are the creative power behind change. Every action starts with a thought, a desire and an intention that sets a direction. Whether you want to climb a mountain, set up a charity or cook for a friend, it begins with an intention – a decision fuelled by the desire to make something happen.

How does it work? An intention starts with a mental picture of a change or goal – material, spiritual or physical – that you want in your life. Then it requires focus and action to make your intention real. Think of an intention as the match you strike to make a fire, or the seed you plant into soil. You don't always know how big the flames will be or how high the plant will grow, but you trust that a result will come.

The benefits of intentional living

When you purposefully set intentions, you take responsibility for the outcome. You now know *why* you do what you do, and if it doesn't work, you can set a different intention. You are no longer the victim of circumstance.

Instead of letting the world decide for you, you become the author of your own destiny and decide what you wish to create in your life. What is ultimately important for most people is not accumulated possessions, success and acclaim, but feelings such as love and happiness.

The practice of intention-setting can be very quick. In as little as five minutes a day you can begin to change your whole life and see the benefits – becoming grounded and rooted in your choices, more deeply in touch with your instinct and more at peace.

This sense of positive energy increases if you use the meditation and visualization practices in this book.

So, read on

In this little book I will share with you some questions,
inspirations and practices that you can use to determine
what choices are most authentic and powerful for you.
Through these, I hope you will learn to connect deeply
with life in all its meaning. I want to give you a map that
will show you some of the possibilities you can explore
in your mind, so that you can decide on the direction
of your own journey.

You can either read the book straight through or dip in
and check out sections, as your instinct suggests. Sometimes
we get deep insights when we revisit questions or activities.

My intention is that, by joining me on this journey, you
will be energized and will find a wellspring of happiness,
love, peace and fulfilment every day for the rest of your life.

So dream the greatest dreams you can for yourself. Imagine
what's possible – even impossible. And live to your highest
purpose and your greatest joy.

1. Get Ready

"Happiness is when what you think, what you say and what you do are in harmony."

MAHATMA GANDHI

Take charge of your life

You know that exciting feeling you used to get when you were young and there were presents to be opened on your birthday – that anticipation about what a gift was going to be like? That's what intentional living is like. A change is coming.

This time, the gift giver and the gift receiver are both the same person – you.

So get ready for the promise of what your life can be like and what it will bring you. Because your life can be wonderful.

Luck

Have you ever had times when everything is going
well and you think, "I'm so lucky at the moment"?
Or perhaps, "I wonder if this luck will last?" Or
maybe, "How come others have all the luck?".
Or "Why wasn't I born as lucky as so-and-so?"

Luck is great while it lasts, but ultimately a belief in luck
is disempowering. If you believe in luck, you basically
believe that you can't influence your life. Instead you are
at the whim of some force that you have no power over.
When you live intentionally, *you* are in charge of creating
your own luck. It takes courage to look at yourself in this
way, but it's worth it, because everything you are has
brought you to this exciting moment of change.

Before you can begin to live intentionally there is value in
getting to know yourself as you are now – being mindful
of what's really important to you, celebrating who you are,
discovering what you believe and what you wish to change.
Then you can make a decision about the nature of your
future intentional life.

The four YOUs

We all wear masks to the world and gradually reveal ourselves to people we feel comfortable being vulnerable with. On the following page we will take a closer look at the four different versions of you that are out there in the world.

"The unexamined life
is not worth living."

SOCRATES

1. "The YOU acquaintances know." We generally start relationships carefully, by showing others a curated and superficial version of ourselves. Often we try to make a good impression.

2. "The YOU your friends and family know." This is a more complete and deeper version of you, with some of your flaws and vulnerabilities disclosed.

3. "The YOU only you know." This is the version of you that you may not trust others to accept just yet.

4. "The YOU even you don't know yet." None of us knows ourselves completely. Life and self-examination are the ways to discover things we don't know about ourselves. As you live through different experiences, you will learn more about yourself.

The activities on the next pages are designed to reveal more of yourself to you and, hopefully, to others as well, by encouraging self-exploration, curiosity and an authentic approach to your life.

What is your story?

Let's start at the beginning
– *your* beginning – which is
where you are now. Imagine
what you would say if
someone asked you about
your life, that is, your *story*.
How would you answer
the following questions?

- ◆ Do you feel you are leading
  a life that matters?

- ◆ Have you chosen your life,
  or have you allowed other
  people to choose it for you?

- ◆ Do you know the top
  priorities in your life?

- ◆ Does the life you live
  reflect these priorities?

- ◆ Would you change your
  story, if you could relive it?

Real success

Consider some of the successful people who have had a powerful impact on the world. You might believe they had such strong support throughout their lives that they were always destined to have a life that mattered. In fact, the opposite is often true.

Many of the people we look up to suffered early lives full of poverty or hardship. Winston Churchill was neglected by his family; Maya Angelou endured abuse and racial prejudice; Florence Nightingale suffered from depression. What they shared was enormous resilience and a reason to go on being in charge of their own destiny.

Of course, not all of us are going to change the world so obviously. Not all of us want to. But each of us matters in life. We all have a finite time on this Earth in which to make a difference to our own and other people's lives. We can all live with purpose, if we set an intention to discover what matters.

Your impact on the world

If you come into contact with one person a day –
every day of your life – you will meet tens of
thousands of people in your lifetime. You can't
not influence the world. Your very presence on
this Earth has an effect on it.

This is illustrated in the classic movie *It's a Wonderful Life*.
George Bailey, the suicidal hero, is given the opportunity
by his guardian angel to see what would happen to the
world without him in it. He is shown that each life
touches many other lives, without us even realizing it.

We probably won't know exactly what hole we would leave
if we weren't on this Earth, but we can set an intention to
take personal responsibility for our thoughts and actions, and
opt for a life that works for others, as well as for ourselves.

ACTIVITY
What's really important?

This activity will help you discover what's important to you *now*. What do you want to change and what do you want to keep? This exercise helps you to eliminate noise and clutter and focus on what's really essential to you.

The key to answering all the questions (here and elsewhere in this book) is to be honest with yourself. Remember: you never have to show your answers to anyone else.

Think about the different areas of your life:

 Family   💎 Personal development

💎 Relationships   💎 Spiritual development

 Career   💎 Other

 Social impact

Then start to jot down some ideas for each area, using the page opposite as a template.

WHAT DO I WANT TO...

> _STOP?_

> _START?_

> _CONTINUE?_

> _EXPERIENCE MORE OF?_

> _WHAT WILL I FEEL MORE OF WHEN I MAKE THESE CHANGES?_

Be, do, have

Most of us approach life with a HAVE, DO, BE mentality. "When I HAVE enough time, then I'll DO the things I want, then I'll BE happy." The problem with this is that you are always waiting for something to change for you, in the same way someone may rely on luck (see page 14).

The intentional approach is to ask yourself, "Who will I BE when I have achieved my goal?" By acting as if you are already this person you will naturally DO the things such a person does, which will allow you to HAVE what you want.

Consider what it is important to BE, DO or HAVE in your life. Look at the lists you compiled for pages 20–1 and answer the following questions:

💎 What do I *really mean* by this? (The more specific you can be, the better.)

💎 *Why* is this important to me? (The more you can hook into the reasons *why* you want to make changes, the more likely you are to make them happen.)

💎 Which of these are *critical* to me?

💎 What will happen when my life has all of this in it?

How beliefs equal life

Do you believe that: you *can* change your life;
you *are able* to live according to your own rules;
it's *okay* to live according to your own rules?

You can only create or change what you *believe* you can
create or change.

 Our beliefs about life form our thoughts.

Our words and actions spring from these thoughts
(conscious or unconscious).

Our daily actions turn into habits after a while.

Your character will be formed and judged by you, and
others, according to your words, actions and habits. The
person you become will guide your eventual destiny. So be
careful with what you choose to believe and think. If your
destiny is heading in a direction you don't like, then it's time
to change your thoughts, your intentions and, through this,
your actions, your words, your character and your life.

Seven empowering beliefs for intentional living

Beliefs are either empowering or disempowering. Why not adopt these seven empowering beliefs, instead of any disempowering ones?

1. *Power lies inside you.* You have the power, through your thoughts and intentions, to change your life.

2. *You have all the gifts and resources that you need right now.* The power to change starts with the intentions that you set today. Your future need not be ruled by the past.

3. *What you believe will become the truth of your life.* Your intentions create the reality, and what you focus on is what you will create. Consciously setting intentions will change the outcomes you get.

4. *Limits exist only in your mind.* Change your mindset and you will alter your experience of life.

5. *The outcome of your intentions shows you what they really are.* If you're not creating the life you want, change your intentions.

6. *People always make the best choices available to them at the time.* We aren't perfect, and it doesn't matter if you change your intentions later on. Learning is part of life.

7. *Those who are the most flexible will create the best outcomes.* Continually renew and reset your intentions. Keep examining what really matters. All life is essentially feedback.

2. Discover

> "Everything rests
> on the tip of intention."
>
> TIBETAN PROVERB

Identify your purpose

Intentional living is a process of self-discovery and of conscious choices about what will bring most joy, purpose and inner peace to your life.

Human beings spend much of their time fulfilling basic needs – food, shelter and survival. Once these are satisfied, our lives are empty unless we can identify what is important to us and then actually go and live by it. Otherwise, it won't matter how much money, power or influence we have, as we still won't be living a life that truly matters.

A few years ago I met an amazing couple who had fostered hundreds of children over 30 years. They weren't rich or famous, but they were fulfilled. They thought they were selfish, because their choices had brought them so much love, but everything they received, they also gave to others.

Having a purpose in life is an incredible gift. The greatest gifts are those that can be shared: like the gift of love.

The gifts of intentional living

An intentional existence should bring positive feelings into your life, such as:

- Joy
- Fulfilment
- Happiness
- Gratitude
- Serenity
- Bliss
- Inner peace
- Harmony
- Awe
- Motivation
- Love

What feelings do you want more of?

What's the best feeling you could possibly experience?

Take a sheet of paper and write down all the ideas you have. Assume that life and the universe want you to experience good feelings, so don't limit yourself. Refer to this list frequently and add to it whenever you want.

How can I serve the world?

Give positive energy to the world and you will receive it back multiple times.

But how – and what – do you wish to give back?

Do you wish to give to the
environment? To your neighbours?
Do you want to show love and
compassion to your family?
Bring joy and laughter?
Serve charitably?
Give materially?

My purpose

We make choices every day. Ten years later we may look back at them and realize that many of them didn't matter all that much. The trick is to work out what the biggest thing is that will change your life for the better over the long term, and then focus on it.

So find a quiet place and ask yourself:

 What does my heart most desire?

 What do I most want to express in my life?

 What are my priorities in the next part of my life?

 What would a life aligned with those priorities look like?

Now think about how this translates to a sense of purpose to guide your life:

 What is the single most important thing I can work toward that will give me a sense of purpose?

 How can I bring meaning and that sense of purpose into my everyday life?

If you're not sure, ask yourself this question:

 What is the *one* thing I can do that would change the world for the better more than *anything* else?

You may have fully formed or half-formed thoughts or merely the seeds of ideas. Wherever you are right now in your thinking is exactly where you should be. The next exercises will help you focus more on what really matters. You can choose the one that most appeals to you or you can try them all.

Your ideal self

We all have a best version of ourselves in our heads. This ideal self uses the gifts it receives every day from life and also gives out to others. What is your ideal self like?

The only reason you aren't your ideal self is because you haven't done those things *yet*. Maybe you live inside your comfort zone. You may feel it's too big a risk or not worth the effort to change, or perhaps you feel you can never achieve this version of yourself. Or you simply haven't realized until now that you can take this opportunity to change. The chance for moving in a new direction in life is always there. In fact, it's *here*. Right now.

What will your life as a whole be like, when you are this best version of yourself?

What do you need to change, to make your ideal life your *actual* life?

What will your very first step be, when you decide to become your ideal self?

Your ideal day

One of the best ways of figuring out if something is really right for you is to imagine and describe your future days, weeks and months as if you are living this new life already.

Imagine yourself living a life that matters.

- Where are you? What sort of place do you live in?

- What do you say to yourself? What do others say to you?

- Who do you see during the day?

- What time do you get up?

- What types of things do you do with your day?

- How healthy are you?

- Are you busier or less busy?

- What is the biggest change? What is the same?

- How do you feel?

Write down anything that occurs to you.

The 100-year-old you

This task connects you with a "future imaginary you" who can act as a guide to your unconscious mind, helping you to tap into your intuition.

Sit quietly. Make sure you are not going to be disturbed. Imagine you are 100 years old. You have lived a long, happy and fulfilled life. You have made a positive impact on the world. What gave you most joy? What gift did you bring to the world? What will you be remembered for? Take a few moments to write down your thoughts.

Now, imagine that the *future you* can travel back to talk to the *younger you* sitting here right now. What positive advice would you give to the *younger you* about what you could learn or know?

Finally, imagine there is a path between the *younger you* and the *future you*. You are laying down stepping stones along this path and each stone is an intention or an action.

Write down at least three future steps that take you toward this fulfilled 100-year-old you.

My virtual mentor

We don't all have real mentors who can help us get where we want to go in life, but imaginary ones can be just as effective. By thinking of someone with qualities you really admire, you can ask them questions in your head and imagine how they would respond to circumstances that you encounter.

Your inspiration doesn't need to be someone you know or have met. It could be a leader or star in their field, someone from history or even from fiction, or you can *imagine* what sort of person you would admire and the passion and purpose they would have.

When you need a mentor, visualize this person sitting in front of you. What advice or wisdom would they give you?

ACTIVITY

The diamond in the mist visualization

This is a wonderful way to get your imagination going and let your right brain – your creative brain – play its part in determining your future. Seeing positive imagery in your mind's eye is great for clarifying what you want and for motivating you to start taking action toward your goals.

1. Imagine that you own a powerful telescope. When you look through it, you can see a priceless diamond in the distance, glinting in the sun. You know it is the most precious object in all the world and, when you look at it, you feel incredible. However, in order to reach it, you need to cross a vast river and climb a mountain.

2. Just as you decide to start the journey, a thick mist descends, so that you are no longer able to see the diamond or the obstacles in the way. But you know it is still possible to reach the diamond, and that you will do whatever it takes to do so.

3. And so you begin your journey with happiness in your heart, ready to overcome whatever obstacles your adventure brings.

What is your diamond? What is so important to you that it will keep you going, even when you stumble in the mist?

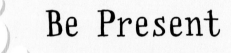

3. Be Present

"Vision is the art of seeing things invisible."

JONATHAN SWIFT

Focus on your intentions

We live in a noisy, busy world. Cutting through the daily distractions and taking time to be quiet and still allows you to access your intuition and look at what's really important to your wellbeing, both now and in the future.

Being still, being mindful or meditating is a way of entering an alpha state – a deeper state of mind – where you can most easily access your higher truth and be truly present in the moment. This is a place of great power where you can gain wisdom and set your intentions.

Meditation, mindfulness and visualization are all different words, but similar practices. They involve being still for a few moments, relaxing the mind and body and breathing more deeply, while focusing on one thing. The basics are very simple to learn. Some meditations are done to music, some to words and others in silence; some sitting, some standing and others lying down. All of these are valid, so do experiment to find what works best for you.

The benefits of silence

You don't have to be religious or spiritual to practise meditation, but over thousands of years most spiritual disciplines have taught stillness and calmness, because of their many benefits.

The metaphysical system of Huna – which is thought to derive from Hawaiian practice, and from which my own empowering beliefs are adapted – is just one of the traditions that believes that, through entering the meditative state, a clear channel is opened between the Higher Self and the unconscious, bringing greater self-knowledge and insight.

Research shows that meditation is good for you. The benefits of regularly accessing the alpha state are increased clarity, reduced stress and a better perspective on life. When we are still, our breathing becomes deeper, bringing health benefits, too. All breath is energy, so when you breathe in, you breathe in energy. When you breathe out, you breathe out stress. Many people believe that meditation also has anti-aging benefits.

Creating a quiet inner space

From the point of view of intentional living, you can use stillness and quiet to discover what is important to you, free from the noise and distractions of daily life. You can also create a quiet inner space in order to set and review your intentions. In this chapter you will find different practices that you can use to focus, begin to open your mind and heart, find inner peace and access your inner wisdom.

ACTIVITY

Observing the breath

When we are rushing around, many of us have a tendency to breathe from the chest. Stopping and letting your breath settle will bring it down to the stomach and relax your whole body. Being in the moment begins with healthy breathing.

Do the following exercise as many times as you like through the day, for as long as you like. The more you are mindful of your breath, the more you will give yourself the space to get in touch with yourself.

1. Standing or sitting, find a posture of stillness.

2. Close your mouth, so that you are breathing through your nose.

3. Focus on your nose and your breathing. Observe the breath coming in and out of your body. You don't need to consciously breathe in and out; just notice your breath.

4. As you relax your body, feel your mind settling down. Enjoy the positive feelings flowing into your body. Stay in this place of inner calm for as long as you like.

ACTIVITY

Connecting with your Higher Self

Opening your third eye is a way of connecting with your inner wisdom, or what some traditions call your "Higher Self". The third eye – also known as the inner eye – is located in the space between the eyebrows and is also the seat of the sixth chakra, or vortex of energy.

By activating this energy centre regularly, you will find that you achieve heightened intuition. Ideally, meditate at a similar time each day to build a new habit. With practice, you can spend 10–15 minutes enjoying this meditation.

1. Find somewhere you won't be disturbed. Either sit cross-legged on the floor with a straight back, or on a chair with your feet planted firmly on the ground. Place your hands on your lap, with your palms facing upward.

2. Close your eyes. Relax your whole body and let your breath settle in your stomach by breathing very slowly in through the nose and out through the nose three times.

3. With your eyes still closed, look up at your third eye. Focus gently on this point. Initially you may be aware of darkness, but then you may see a white or purple light or experience an image in your mind's eye. This means that you have activated your third eye.

Laozi

One of my favourite stories comes from the Chinese sage Laozi. He believed that what is soft conquers what is hard. When the wind blows, it knocks down tall, strong-looking trees, but soft grass bends and survives.

This ancient wisdom teaches us about the attitude that we should take in life. Intentional living is about "soft focus", not hard resolve or willpower.

Accessing your inner wisdom

This is a simple method you can use, for a few minutes at a time, to become familiar with getting in touch with your intuition.

1. Sit or lie down somewhere you won't be disturbed. Close your eyes.

2. Take three deep breaths through your nose, breathing in very slowly and letting the air out very slowly.

3. Now allow your body to relax. One easy way to do this is to begin with the tips of your toes and move up to the top of your head, deliberately tensing and letting go of each part of your body in turn. So clench your toes as tightly as possible and then let go, then your calves, thighs, stomach, chest, arms, hands and face. Eventually you will be relaxed, with every part of your body loose and limp.

4. Next, imagine walking down ten steps, relaxing more deeply with every breath and with every step.

5. At the bottom of the steps is a door. On the other side you will find a sanctuary – the most relaxing place in the world. This could be a beach, a garden or a forest. The choice is yours. Notice the beautiful smells and sounds.

6. Stay as long as you like here, relaxing. You can imagine making it even more special, perhaps by playing on the sand, planting beautiful flowers or a tree.

7. If you wish, ask for a message.

8. Imagine a light coming from somewhere in the distance. Approach the light. Bathe in its glorious warm, vibrant glow, sense it filling up your spirit with joy and happiness.

9. You see a gift waiting for you. Take it, knowing that either now or in the future your intuition will interpret it for you.

10. When you are ready, leave this special place, close the door and climb the steps, knowing that you are bringing the light with you for the rest of the day and longer.

4. Appreciate

"The only thing we have power over in the universe is our own thoughts."

RENÉ DESCARTES

Acknowledge your past

You – and everyone on this planet – deserve
to live a life of significance that brings joy and
blessings to the world. You are truly worthy of
a happy, fulfilled and harmonious life. This is part
of the gift you were given at birth by the universe.

You may have had difficulties in the past: an unhappy
childhood, illness, pain or a lack of love. You are not alone.
Life is full of obstacles, but the great power we have as
human beings is to forgive what has happened, be grateful
for what we have learned and move on with purpose.

When you *truly* let go of the past, you don't cloud your
future intentions with hurt and pain. Instead, you start
a new journey, leaving the old baggage behind.

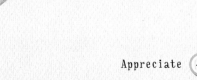

The gift of gratitude

Gratitude is one of the greatest gifts you can offer yourself. A thankful heart brings happiness and is open to opportunities. When you focus on the good things that are happening in your life, you bring more of them to you.

Next time you experience anything – either pleasant or unpleasant – stop, take a breath and say to yourself, "Thank you. Thank you for what I have learned and experienced."

Through this simple ritual you can change your consciousness and see what you experience not as good or bad, but as a blessing, because everything you experience helps you to define and refine your purpose.

Life is a series of choices. You can't choose what people or circumstances you encounter, but you can choose your reaction to whatever comes across your path. One of the truest sayings is "The past is the past; you can only influence the present and the future." Every step you take, however small, is a step in a particular direction. The direction that you choose, and the actions and reactions you have, are under *your* control. This is what intentional living is all about.

When you become actively grateful for life in all its aspects, you are no longer some passive recipient of luck, which is thrown out from time to time in your direction by the universe. Instead, you are in charge of your reaction. You consciously choose, and intend to use, all your experiences to build a meaningful, harmonious life.

> "Don't set your mind on things you don't possess as if they were yours, but count the blessings you actually possess."

MARCUS AURELIUS

Gratitude journal

Numerous studies have demonstrated the benefits of keeping a gratitude journal. People who practise gratitude feel more optimistic and have better physical and psychological health. It encourages you to focus on the positive things in your life.

So take a moment, find a quiet spot and reflect on your day.

- Write down at least five things you are grateful for today: it could be people, events or experiences.

- How did you contribute to these things happening, or being, in your life?

- Write, or say to yourself, "I am grateful for…" and list all the positive things you have just noted.

- Similarly, think about all the different areas of your life: the people you know, the places you go, what you do, what you have and what you are.

- What are you grateful for? How have you contributed to these things happening, or being, in your life?

- Write, or say to yourself, "I am grateful for…" and list all the positive things you have just noted.

Write a letter

In this digital age of emails, instant messaging and emojis, it has become rarer to receive a handwritten card. Writing takes effort, which is why it is a sure-fire way to show someone how much they mean to you.

Why not write a card or letter to someone who has been kind to you and give it to them face to face? You will be passing on gratitude with intent and meaning.

Think about who you are grateful to. What specifically did they do that affected you? Tell them how and why it made a difference. Even a few lines can help make someone's day.

Forgive

Forgiveness of past pain and the acceptance of loss makes us powerful. The 2nd-century CE Roman emperor Marcus Aurelius reminds us that we can't be hurt by the unpleasant things in life, because we can forgive people and love them, as we "were born to work together, like a man's two hands".

None of us can go through life separate from others and, unless you are a saint, it is likely there will be some times when other people throw you off-balance. An important part of intentional living is to forgive. Forgiveness is a powerful tool, because by forgiving others for hurt or pain in the past or present, you release that pain and allow happiness to replace it.

If you set your intentions from a place of pain, all you will get back is more pain. If you set your intentions from a place of hurt, you will receive back more hurt. In fact, the old magical adage rings true: "One finger points out and three fingers point back." For every emotion you project to the world, you will get it back threefold.

If you are not sure what you believe about life, then look around you. "Like attracts like" – what this means is that

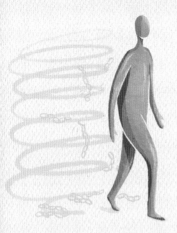

> "To be wronged is nothing unless you continue to remember it."
>
> CONFUCIUS

emotions are contagious. A happy person tends to be surrounded by other happy people; a peaceful person by other peaceful people. Just by existing in the world, we impact upon others.

We often hold other people to higher standards than those that we would hold for ourselves. We notice faults in others that we forgive in ourselves. We can't move forward while we hold pictures in our mind surrounded by negative energy from the past. Forgiveness is a way of separating someone's behaviour from the person. It doesn't mean that you forget what happened in the past, but you do forgive the mistake and move on.

ACTIVITY

Forgiveness and letting go of negativity

This exercise is adapted from a Hawaiian forgiveness practice and is a powerful way to absolve another person – and to be forgiven by them.

1. Close your eyes. Hold a picture of a particular person from your present or past in your mind, as if you are looking at them on a stage below and in front of you. Notice a slim silver cord attaching you to them. Through this link you hold all the words, actions and experiences that have passed between the two of you.

2. Notice whether you hold positive or negative feelings about this person, or perhaps both.

3. Ask yourself: have I thanked them for the good things they have brought into my life? If not, you can do so now.

4. Do you have anything you need to be forgiven for by them? Or need to forgive them for? This is your chance to say anything that was never said.

5. Thank them for what you have learned by their presence in your life. Appreciate the growth this has brought you.

6. Allow the person to say to you whatever they need to say. Take this opportunity to say, "I'm sorry for anything I did or didn't say, did or didn't do, that caused you any pain."

7. Bring to mind the positive feelings of what it has been like to forgive someone in the past or imagine how wonderful it can feel to forgive. Say, "I forgive you." Imagine the person forgiving you. Doing this is a powerful way of letting go of the energy that negative memories can hold in our psyches.

8. Ask the person on the stage, "Do you support me to be the best version of myself?" Notice their reply.

9. Imagine that you have a sword made of white light. Use it to cut the cord between you. In so doing, let go of any old issues. Imagine the cords reabsorbing back into both of you. The next time you think of this person with love, a shiny new cord – free of past attachments – will form.

10. Allow the other person to leave the stage and, as you complete this process in your mind, surround yourself and the other person with light. Light is a powerful metaphor for letting go of negativity and bad thoughts and moving forward with kindness, joy and compassion.

5. Get Set, Go!

"Let yourself be silently drawn by the strange pull of what you really love. It will not lead you astray."

RUMI

Align your intentions

Get ready to begin living intentionally. The intentions that you set now will determine where you focus your energy and time – both in the present and in the future.

Over the years I have done a lot of research into different goal-setting and intention practices. One of the great lessons I have learned is that every wish and every choice has consequences. And it is important that, in the choices you make for yourself, you also consider the wider impact.

This is not the same as taking someone else's path. Instead, it is what is referred to as being "aligned" in your choices. Life can go very wrong if you only take into account one part of your life and fail to consider the other parts. This is what happens to the successful millionaire who keeps getting divorced, or the person who sets up a charity, but falls out with their own family.

So choose your intentions with care and respect for all beings on this planet, including yourself.

My BIG intention for my life

Make sure all your intentions take account of what you wish both to receive from the universe and give back to the world. Remember, it is helpful to set intentions for your life as a whole, as well as on a daily basis or for a specific event.

Write down or say aloud:

💎 "My intention is…"

💎 "This is important to me because…"

💎 "My first step toward this is…"

How to say an intention

When you write or say an intention, you should use the present or present continuous tense. This is powerful, because it projects you in your imagination into this future version of yourself and your life:

🔹 "My intention is…"

🔹 "I now am…"

🔹 "I now have…"

🔹 "I am now doing…"

🔹 "I am now having…"

🔹 "I am now believing…"

Imagining that you have already achieved what you want is an acknowledgment that thought guides actions. Before you achieve you must believe and conceive. Using the present tense lets your brain know this isn't just a "want" any more but a decision. It's a done deal. You've started the journey.

Why not set an intention to be kind?

The Buddhist monk and peace marcher Maha Ghosananda, who was known as the "Gandhi of Cambodia", said that a peaceful heart springs from being open-hearted and compassionate. A peaceful person makes other people peaceful.

What Maha Ghosananda reveals is that compassion and peace are contagious. One person at peace can make a peaceful world, because every intention that we have impacts both upon ourselves and others. This, in turn, impacts upon the wider community and the world. The intention of Buddhism, as well as other spiritual traditions, is to be gentle, forgiving and kind.

If you want others to treat you with consideration and kindness, it starts with you. Think through the impact of your intentions as much as you can. Consider what it will be like if your intentions come from kindness to the world. Won't that bring you more joy, happiness and love?

The world isn't always what we want it to be. It's filled with hardship, pain and even war. But we *can* choose our thoughts and actions. We can set an intention to be kind, not cruel.

We can decide to wake up each morning and find happiness in whatever the day brings, and gratitude at the end of the day for whatever the day has brought.

You don't need to be angry when you encounter anger. You don't need to seek revenge or retribution. Set an intention to face the world with understanding and kindness and you are more likely to find inner peace.

Bring intention into every area of your life

Consider the different areas of your life. Look at the lists you already made concerning what is important to you (see page 20). Consider the following:

💎 How do you want to grow as a person?

💎 What do you want to give back?

💎 What might other people most appreciate?

💎 What kind of challenge would help you grow?

💎 How would you like to develop creatively?

Write down specific intentions for each area of your life (see opposite). Which of these areas are really important to you? Which will bring happiness to you and those around you?

YOUR FAMILY

YOUR RELATIONSHIPS

YOUR HEALTH AND FITNESS

ADVENTURE

SPIRITUAL GROWTH

CREATIVITY

CONTRIBUTION TO THE WORLD (PEOPLE, ENVIRONMENT, WELLBEING)

A quick check

Here are some questions that you can ask yourself to make sure all your choices are aligned. Think about a particular intention that you have set, then ask yourself what it will bring into your life.

- Will it be good for me?

- Will it be good for my family?

- Will it be good for the world as a whole?

- What will the consequences be for other areas of my life?

- Will it bring more balance into my life?

- Will it bring more happiness to me?

- Will it bring more fulfilment into my life?

- What will happen if I don't act on this intention?

- What will happen if I do act on this intention?

- What *won't* happen if I do act on this intention?

- What *won't* happen if I don't act on this intention?

Letting go of over-attachment

To live an intentional life, you have to want things to happen, but, if you want something too much, it can prevent it occurring.

An intention is not the same as an obsession or an addiction. It is not the same as a need, a "should" or a "must". It is a decision that you can change.

How do you know whether you are attached, or unattached, to the outcome of an intention? Think about your intention, then ask yourself these questions:

 If this intention doesn't work out in the way I want it to, can I set a new intention and move forward?

 If this intention doesn't give me the outcome I want, can I learn what to do, or ask for it differently, and move forward?

 If this intention doesn't give me the outcome I want, am I happy to learn what I need to learn about myself, in order to restate my intention in a different way?

 Am I happy to remain curious about my intentions rather than rigid about them?

Take action

An intention is just the beginning. It means nothing if you don't take action. You will only get your diamond if you take the first step into the mist, cross rivers and climb mountains (see pages 36–7) and trust that you are on the right path.

We can all wish good to the world and happiness for ourselves, but wanting and wishing are not the same as intending. Wanting is passive. Intentional living is an *active* practice and habit that you commit to every day.

Each day when you awake, make sure you intend
to take a step forward in alignment with your
highest intentions. Let your sense of purpose flow
into your daily routines and bring you joy.

ACTIVITY

Seven steps for setting intentions

Follow these steps to help establish your intentions, visualize them and then integrate them into your daily life. Remember to retain enough flexibility to let the universe take care of the specifics.

1. Adopt beliefs that will empower you.

2. Decide what you want to change.

3. Be still. Find a moment of calm and centre yourself. This will get easier the more you practise.

4. State your intention clearly, using the present tense. Think about what you are in the process of *being*, *doing* and *having* – for instance, "I now am…", "I am now doing…", "I now have…" (see page 22).

5. Imagine what it will be like to succeed in your intention. Visualize it and feel it as if it already exists, like a memory in the future. What will you feel like when this intention actualizes? Remember to banish all doubt or criticism of yourself or others.

6. Detach yourself from the outcome. Trust — trust that you don't need to force anything or fight for anything.

7. Take action. Integrate your intentions into your daily life by acting as if they are definitely going to happen. You don't need to be rigid about this. A soft focus will help your intentions become a reality. Let the universe take care of the how and when.

ACTIVITY

Intention rituals

Every day is a new beginning and an opportunity to set intentions that will support your sense of purpose, happiness and wellbeing. These exercises will help you to begin, and end, each day with conscious intention.

Morning

Do this activity when you have just woken and are still in the alpha state of mind – a relaxed and powerful level of consciousness that is equivalent to a meditative state.

1. Take a few moments to be still. Let your mind wonder happily about the day ahead. *How would I like to feel today?*

2. Reflect on your intentions for the day. *How can I move forward today in a way that is aligned with my positive purpose?* Imagine the day being a really positive, happy one.

3. Ask yourself, *How can I bring positive energy to the people I meet today, and to the world as a whole?*

4. Set your intentions for the day. You may want to make a written note to remind yourself to check in with them.

Evening

Here are six powerful questions to help you to stay
on track at the end of the day. Ask yourself:

1. Have I kept to my intentions today?

2. What am I grateful for today?

3. What has made me happy today?

4. What did I do today to act toward my highest purpose?

5. Have I acted toward others and myself with kindness
   and compassion today?

6. What have I given today?

6. Renew

"As long as you live,
keep learning how to live."

SENECA

Renew your intention regularly

It's easy to get enthusiastic about new ideas and then for all that enthusiasm to disappear after a few months, or even weeks or days. Once you have incorporated intentions into your life, how do you sustain your motivation to live in this way?

Intentional living is a process of daily focus about the path you will take in life. In this chapter you will find some inspiration to help you stay on track. Keep refreshing, renewing and resetting your intentions, and use what happens in your life as feedback on your intentions so far.

A period of
intentional living

By giving yourself a period of time in which to
build the habit of intentional living, you get used
to seeing – and feeling – how your life improves.

Start with one week. Set your intentions for the next seven
days. At the end of seven days, review the actions you took
and what happened in your life. What would you keep the
same or do differently? Have your positive feelings increased?

My year of intentional living

This plan is more ambitious (see the sample on pages 78–9).
Get a notebook or a wall planner – or create your own
spreadsheet. Ensure it is appealing enough for you to want
to look at, and keep returning to, all year. Choose a period
of time: if a year is too long, try three or six months.

 Write down your overall purpose: the one big intention
you want to make sure you keep sight of.

 Now look at the areas of your life that are potentially
most impacted by this, and where you want to create
change: for instance, your relationships, your family,

your health and wellbeing. Suppose you have three areas and three months: you can choose to focus on each area for a month, setting out the intentions that will really improve this area of your life and bring you more happiness and a greater sense of purpose. Of course you are not going to focus on one area for a month and then stop, but creating intentions for a fixed period of time will embed new habits and give you a good start. You can then add in extra intentions later in the year.

 Write down your big intention for the month, then split it up into further smaller goals that you are going to take action on over the coming month.

 Now take your first action.

Intentional year sample plan

MY *BIG* INTENTION

I AM NOW HELPING NEGLECTED ANIMALS BY SETTING UP AN ANIMAL SANCTUARY.

🦴 JANUARY - EDUCATION

Big intention: to learn about animal welfare.

MONTHLY ACTIONS

- ❯ Sign up for a class
- ❯ Attend every Monday
- ❯ Complete my certification

FEBRUARY - *HEALTH AND WELLBEING*

Big intention: to get healthy, so that I have the energy to do what I love.

MONTHLY ACTIONS

❥ Join a gym

❥ Run every Tuesday

❥ Do a yoga class three times a week

❥ Drink eight glasses of water a day

MARCH - *HELPING ANIMALS*

Big intention: to create time away from work to volunteer at a local shelter.

MONTHLY ACTIONS

❥ Work from home two days a week

❥ Volunteer once a week, to begin with

❥ Put an hour in my diary today for work on my plan for the sanctuary

Take 15 minutes

It's easy to start something and then run out
of enthusiasm. That's where the "power of 15"
comes into play. Give yourself 15 minutes to do
something – no more, no less. This is powerful,
because anyone can spare 15 minutes in a day.

For example, give yourself 15 minutes to prepare a healthy
salad, if you want to lose weight; 15 minutes to research new
jobs; 15 minutes to clear out your wardrobe; or 15 minutes
to plan your first novel.

We don't become better at things automatically. We learn and
grow through incremental steps. The power of 15 minutes is
great because it hooks you in. You have taken action toward
what you want to achieve, without running out of steam.

By thinking in short time-bursts you will retain your
enthusiasm for the task at hand. Your desire to continue
along this path will grow and grow.

If you need to ask for help from someone else, start by
asking *them* for 15 minutes. Most people will have that
small amount of time to spare.

3 × 15 = success

💎 After your first 15 minutes, stop and take a break.

💎 Do another 15 minutes. Stop and reward yourself.

💎 Then do another 15 minutes.

Now, how much do you want to carry on? Probably far more than when you first thought about your task.

Declutter your life

If you think you don't have enough time to focus on your intentions, declutter your life. Many of us accumulate clutter over time, so think about what you want to keep that fits with your intentions for your new life, and get rid of stuff that doesn't.

Start with your home. How much stuff do you *actually* use or need? Look at your books, clothes, pots and pans, and so on. Get into the habit of throwing out stuff regularly – it will clear your environment and your mind at the same time. For a week, see how many things you can get rid of, and how much lighter you feel afterward. Then do another week.

Take a look at your friendships. Are you hanging onto friendships for the sake of them? Are they going to support you in the next stage of your meaningful life? Think about who is really special to you and spend more time with them.

Start saying No. Say No to unimportant stuff. Say No to the things you don't want to do. Notice whether you have difficulty saying No. If you do, set the intention to learn to say No by practising. Practice is the way to every new habit.

Intentional moments

One quick way to create a truly impactful life for yourself or others lies in the small moments. You can intentionally create little moments of joy, kindness or compassion every day and thereby weave a purposeful life. Below are two examples. Maybe you can think of others?

◇ Carry out a random act of kindness each day for a week: help a friend; give to charity; buy a stranger a coffee.

◇ Take time to talk to others: look away from your smartphone and connect with a stranger or reconnect with a friend. Notice how good you feel afterward.

Nudge theory

Human beings are imperfect. We are not rational robots that always make the right choices. We plan to do things, but struggle to find the time. We don't always prioritize what is important over what demands our immediate attention. That's why you can look back over the course of a whole year – or even a decade – and wonder what you have achieved during that time.

Two American professors, Richard Thaler and Cass Sunstein, are responsible for the increasing popularity of nudge theory. They understood that to help people make good decisions, a nudge in the right direction is often all that is required.

How can you use nudge theory to keep your intentions on track? One way is by giving yourself simple reminders.

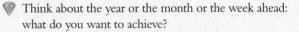 Think about the year or the month or the week ahead: what do you want to achieve?

 Write your aims on a calendar. Now think about the first steps you are going to take to *act* on your intentions.

◆ Set up reminder alarms ahead of these steps, to automatically keep you on track. It is a good idea to give yourself a nudge on the day itself, and halfway through the week or month.

◆ If, for some reason, you go off track because of unforeseen circumstances, reset your nudges, so that you can get back on track as quickly as possible.

Stay curious

None of us has a perfect life, but we can create luck by staying curious about life. Some people know immediately what their purpose is and are able to map out their journey toward it. But many of us discover our purpose bit by bit, through exploration, experimentation and curiosity.

An intentional life is governed by a purpose, but that purpose isn't fixed. It's fluid, responsive and can be changed. It's okay to change your mind. If you aren't getting the results you want in life, through the intentions you have set and the actions you have taken, change something.

Every result is feedback to the curious. Use this feedback to change your mind, alter your intentions and amend your actions.

Explore who you are.

Learn more about yourself every day.

Reset, renew, refresh.

Stay soft

Remember the river
and mountain that
stood in the way of you
reaching that diamond
(see page 36)? Obstacles
can seem daunting, terrible
things, but obstacles can
make us stronger, smarter
and more determined.

When you live an
intentional life, an obstacle
is something to learn from.
Your most valuable insights
about yourself, your own life
and other people don't come from a smooth-flowing
life; they spring from a life full of learning and curiosity.

The next time you encounter an obstacle in an area
of your life, ask yourself, "What is there to learn here?
When I learn this, how will I benefit?" Your attitude
will also determine how you see obstacles.

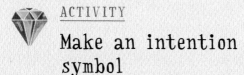

ACTIVITY

Make an intention symbol

This is a great way to remind yourself of your intention.

Get hold of some child's modelling clay – the kind you can mould without baking. Then set aside some quiet time. Do this exercise somewhere where it doesn't matter if you make a mess.

1. Think of one of your intentions.

2. As you do so, hold the clay and start making a shape. Let your intuition guide you. Do this as though it is a form of meditation, but using touch instead of the mind.

3. The shape you make will become a symbol of your intention. You can paint it or further refine it.

4. When it is dry, leave the symbol somewhere you can see it every day.

ACTIVITY

Create a vision board

It's fun to make a vision board, and if you hang it somewhere you can see it every day, it will act as a prompt for you to revisit existing intentions and set new ones.

1. Assemble your materials. You will need a large piece of cardboard or board, glue or pins and scissors.

2. Gather together pictures that represent what you want to bring into your life – pictures relating to career, love, travel, learning, future achievements, and so on. You can cut out images from magazines or search for pictures on the internet or from other sources.

3. Choose images that are colourful and that you *really* like. If they don't make you feel inspired, discard them.

4. Lay your pictures out on your vision board. Step back and check: do these pictures capture your dreams and intentions? Attach the pictures to your board in a collage.

5. Hang your vision board somewhere you will see it daily. And make sure you refresh it as necessary.

Harness your right brain

A vision board helps you to make pleasurable pictures
of the life you wish to create and is a way of making
sure you remember to stay on track with your
intentions. It harnesses the power of your right brain,
which is concerned with creativity, whereas the left
brain is concerned with logic.

The fox and the hedgehog

The ancient Greek poet Archilochus talked about the different natures of foxes and hedgehogs.

A fox is an adaptable and clever creature and has many different strategies for hunting, stealing food and keeping safe. It has many tricks and can adapt itself to numerous situations.

A hedgehog is a simple creature with one trick to survive It is small with spikes and, when it is attacked, it rolls itself into a ball, hoping that its spikes will defend it. It does one thing very well.

To live intentionally, it's good to learn from both of these creatures. Keep a single higher purpose in mind – one big intention (see page 76) – like a hedgehog, but when you face obstacles, learn to be flexible like a fox.

"The fox knows many things, but the hedgehog knows one big thing."

ARCHILOCHUS

Finally...

I hope this little book has begun to bring new ideas and inspiration into your life. Intentional living is a journey. As you step through the mist toward your diamond, step forward with confidence, knowing that wherever you are right now is exactly the right place to begin your journey.

One last thing, before I wish you an amazing intentional life. Life is a team sport and all great endeavours are built with help, even if one person is the star who gets all the glory. When you ask the world for help, it's amazing how the right people just come into your life.

Life isn't a solitary journey. You will always make friends on the way. Other people can help you with ideas and knowledge; they can help you with resources. Your intentions may be deeply personal, but you can still find people to help you on the way. You simply need to ask.

Bon voyage – and happy journeying on your wonderful, curious, experimental new adventure.

"Be happy for
this moment.
This moment
is your life."

OMAR KHAYYÁM

Acknowledgments

To Diana, Sal and Jane. We started this journey together in Hawaii and I am grateful to still have you in my life after all these years. A big shout out to Sarah, too, who is always wise, and to my many teachers and role models over the years, especially Tad, John, Julie, David and Donald.

Thank you also to everyone at Octopus, including the wonderful and professional Leanne, Polly, Juliette and Emily. Thank you to Mandy and Clare for polishing my text. And Abi, your fantastic illustrations bring the ideas to life.

Finally, thank you to my mother, who still teaches me new ideas whenever I speak to her.